Neil Armstrong

Astronaut & First Human to Walk on the Moon

by Grace Hansen

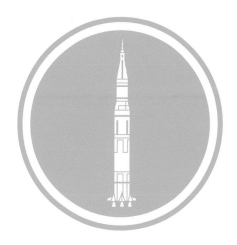

HISTORY MAKER BIOGRAPHIES

Abdo Kids

abdopublishing.com

Published by Abdo Kids, a division of ABDO, P.O. Box 398166, Minneapolis, Minnesota 55439.
Copyright © 2018 by Abdo Consulting Group, Inc. International copyrights reserved in all countries.
No part of this book may be reproduced in any form without written permission from the publisher.
Abdo Kids Jumbo™ is a trademark and logo of Abdo Kids.

102017

012018

 THIS BOOK CONTAINS
RECYCLED MATERIALS

Photo Credits: AP Images, Getty Images, iStock, NASA, Seth Poppel/Yearbook Library
Production Contributors: Teddy Borth, Jennie Forsberg, Grace Hansen
Design Contributors: Dorothy Toth, Laura Mitchell

Publisher's Cataloging in Publication Data

Names: Hansen, Grace, author.

Title: Neil Armstrong: astronaut & first human to walk on the moon / by Grace Hansen.

Other titles: Astronaut & first human to walk on the moon | Astronaut and first human to walk on the
    moon

Description: Minneapolis, Minnesota : Abdo Kids, 2018. | Series: History maker biographies |
    Includes glossary, index and online resource (page 24).

Identifiers: LCCN 2017943149 | ISBN 9781532104282 (lib.bdg.) | ISBN 9781532105401 (ebook) |
    ISBN 9781532105968 (Read-to-me ebook)

Subjects: LCSH: Armstrong, Neil, 1930-2012--Juvenile literature. | Astronauts--United States--
    Biography--Juvenile literature. | Space flight to the moon--Juvenile literature.

Classification: DDC 629.45 [B]--dc23

LC record available at https://lccn.loc.gov/2017943149

Table of Contents

Early Years

Neil Armstrong was born on August 5, 1930. He was born near Wapakoneta, Ohio.

Ohio

Neil was very smart. As a
boy, he became interested
in flying. He had his pilot's
license by the age of 16.

7

In 1947, Neil started college. He went to Purdue University. He studied **aeronautical engineering**.

NEIL ARMSTRONG HALL OF ENGINEERING

Neil Armstrong
BS Aeronautical Engineering 1955
Honorary Doctorate 1970

Joining NASA

Neil served in the navy and finished college. Later, he got a job with the **NACA**. It later became **NASA**. He worked as a test pilot and engineer.

10

Family

In 1956, he married his first wife Janet Shearon. Together they had three children. The family moved to Houston, Texas, in 1963. Neil joined the astronaut program there.

13

Missions & The Moon

On March 16, 1966, Neil went on his first mission. He was the command pilot on **Gemini VIII**. Neil was launched into Earth's orbit for 11 hours.

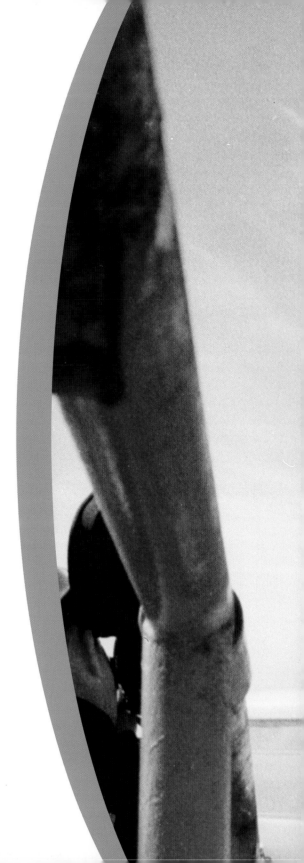

14

Neil's greatest mission came in 1969. On July 16th, Neil and two other men were launched into space. Neil was the mission's commander. He guided the **module** to the moon's surface.

17

At 10:56 p.m. on July 20th, Neil stepped out of the **module**. He said, "That's one small step for man, one giant leap for mankind." He was the first man to walk on the moon!

19

Later Years

Neil stayed at NASA until 1971.

He later became a professor.

Neil died on August 25, 2012,

at the age of 82.

Timeline

Neil begins college at Purdue University.

Neil marries his first wife, Janet. They have 3 children and later divorce. In 1994, he marries his second wife Carol.

March 16
Neil is the command pilot of **Gemini VIII**.

August 25
Neil dies at the age of 82.

1947   **1956**   **1966**   **2012**

1930   **1955**   **1962**   **1969**

August 5
Neil Armstrong is born near Wapakoneta, Ohio.

Neil gets a job at **NACA** as a research pilot.

Neil joins **NASA**'s space program.

July 20
Armstrong is the first man to walk on the moon.

Glossary

aeronautical engineering – a field of engineering that focuses on the development of aircraft and spacecraft.

Gemini VIII – A planned three-day mission where two spacecraft (Gemini and Agena) docked in orbit for the first time. An emergency caused Armstrong to undock and end the mission early.

module – a section of a spacecraft that can detach from the main structure and carry out certain tasks.

NACA – (1915-1958) short for the National Advisory Committee for Aeronautics.

NASA – (1958-present) short for the National Aeronautics and Space Administration.

23

Index

Abdo Kids ONLINE

FREE! ONLINE MULTIMEDIA RESOURCES

Visit **abdokids.com** and use this code to access crafts, games, videos, and more!

Abdo Kids Code:

HNK4282

24